Gregor Mendel

Gregor Mendel

BY **CARLA GREENE**

ILLUSTRATED BY RICHARD CUFFARI

THE DIAL PRESS | NEW YORK

*Many thanks to Pamela Green,
graduate student in genetics at University
of Wisconsin, who read the first draft of the
manuscript and offered valuable suggestions.*

Contents

Johann,
the Peasant Boy

"Look Father, here's a pear from the tree we grafted." The eleven-year-old peasant boy's blue eyes sparkled with pride.

"It's a beauty, Johann," said his father.

"Why do we get better pears when we graft the branch of a strong tree onto a tree that usually bears poor fruit?" Johann asked.

"No one knows that, Johann," said his father. "I suppose it's just nature's way."

The answer did not satisfy the boy. "I hope someone finds out," said Johann. "I would like to know."

7

Johann Mendel was born on July 22, 1822, in Heinzendorf, a village of about fifty cottages, in what was then
Austria, but is now Czechoslovakia. He lived in a small tile-
roofed farmhouse with his parents, Anton and Rosine
Mendel, and his two sisters. Veronika, three years older
than Johann, was a gentle, serious girl who helped her
mother cook plain, wholesome meals and keep house.
Theresia, seven years younger than he, was gay and mis-
chievous. She adored her big brother, who loved to play
hide-and-seek and other games with her.

Most peasants of that day rented their land and were
very poor, but Anton Mendel owned his farm of about
forty-five acres, which was divided into grain, vegetables,
an orchard of fruit trees, and some pasture land for cattle.

8

Nevertheless, it was hard to earn a good living, because instead of paying taxes he had to work three days a week without wages for the lord who had sold him the property. Thus he could only afford coarse clothing and food for his family. There were no luxuries.

Through frugal living, Anton Mendel managed to save a little money because he knew that he would need a dowry for each daughter. His plans for his son were definite. Johann would inherit the farm and live the life of a peasant like his father.

It therefore surprised Anton when his wife told him that Dr. Makitta, the village schoolmaster, had come to visit and told her that Johann had learned all he could in the one local school in Heinzendorf. "He thinks that Johann should go to school at Leipnick now," said Rosine.

"At Leipnick? But that's thirteen miles away. He would need money for room and board."

"We must manage somehow," his wife said softly. "Perhaps we can sell a cow or at least some chickens." Rosine hoped that education would enable Johann to escape the hard life of a peasant. Secretly she wished her son might become a priest, though he had shown no leanings in that direction.

Anton felt that it would be better for Johann to inherit the farm and have something he could depend upon than to take a chance on his future, since career opportunities were scarce in those days. But loving his son deeply, he could not bring himself to deny him the right to an education, which the boy wanted badly. He decided therefore than Johann should go to school at Leipnick for one year, providing he would come home and help on the farm during school vacations. Johann promised that he would.

10

Johann, the Peasant Boy

In the fall of 1833, at the age of eleven, Johann Mendel entered the Leipnick school. He received high marks in all his studies, and his teachers recommended that he go to high school at Troppau, twenty miles from Heinzendorf. The course would take six years.

Johann was not sure his father would agree to the plan. But Anton Mendel had become proud of his son's progress as a student and offered no objections.

So in 1834 Johann entered the Troppau high school. Since money was scarce, as usual, he had to live on a very limited amount of food. Often he was half starved, and he always looked forward to vacations when he could go home and eat as much as he wanted.

Johann's teachers found that he had the bright, inquiring mind of a scientist. He was always asking questions about how living things developed, and why they behaved as they did. The teachers told him what they knew, but their answers did not always satisfy him. There must be better answers, Johann thought. Maybe someday he would find them.

Johann
Receives Bad News

During Johann's fourth year in high school, he received news that his father had been seriously injured. While Anton was working, a rolling log had fallen on his chest and broken two of his ribs.

Johann rushed home. He found his father in severe pain. He offered to give up school and stay home to do the work on the farm. But Anton would not let him.

"You must continue your education," he said, "so you will not have to spend your life doing hard labor as I have had to do."

12

Johann's last two years at Troppau were hard. His father, unable to do much work, could not afford to send him even the small amount of money he had in other years. Johann was often weak from lack of food and found it difficult to study. Every now and then he had to return to the farm to get good meals and build up his strength.

At last, in August, 1840, he finished his six-year course with high marks and received his diploma. This was a very happy occasion for his parents. His mother was especially proud and delighted. She said, "Now you will be important, Johann. You will never have to lead the life of a peasant."

But Johann knew that he needed several more years of study before he would be ready for a career. Upon his teachers' advice, he went to the Philosophical Institute at Olmütz, a fairly large city about one hundred miles from Heinzendorf. He managed to earn a little money from tutoring other students, but the amount was so small that sometimes he had to exist on only bread and butter. In spite of the difficulties, he studied hard and did well. But at times he became desperately discouraged. Then he would go home to the farm for rest and good food.

During his first year at Olmütz, Johann's older sister, Veronika, married a sturdy young peasant, Alois Sturm. Since Anton Mendel was finding it increasingly difficult to work and manage the farm alone, Alois helped him.

The next time Johann came home, his father said:

"I don't think you will ever want to be a farmer, Johann. How would you feel if I turned the farm over to Alois? He handles it so well."

"I think that's a fine idea," said Johann.

Anton told his son that he would provide a small income of ten guldens a year to help him continue his studies. (Ten guldens at that time was worth about one hundred and fifty American dollars.) "I know it is very little," Anton said, "but you know I must still provide a dowry for Theresia."

Theresia, who was almost thirteen, overheard the conversation. She tossed her head and said, "I don't need a dowry. A man will have to marry me for myself. Father, give my dowry to Johann so he can study without starving himself."

"I will not hear of this!" exclaimed Johann. "You are foolish even to think of it."

But Theresia insisted that her dowry be given to her brother right away. Finally seeing that arguments were useless, Johann agreed to accept the money, saying, "I hope and pray that you are right and that I may be able to repay you some day."

A few years later, Theresia, true to her belief in herself, met a fine young man, Leopold Schindler, who loved her enough to marry her without a dowry.

Thanks to his sister's generosity, Johann's second year at Olmütz was much happier. He took courses in philosophy, religion, physics, classical literature, and history. He was a good student in all his subjects but particularly enjoyed studying physics. The physics professor, Father Friedrich Franz, took a warm, friendly interest in his brilliant student.

During his second year at Olmütz, Johann could not reach a decision about his future. After so many years of near starvation and poor health, he did not see how he could go on with his education. What could a young man of twenty with his somewhat limited education do? Teaching positions were not easy to obtain at that time unless one knew someone of influence. He needed some good advice so he went to visit Father Franz.

Father Franz listened to Johann's story, then told him that he had just received a letter from Prelate Cyrill Napp, the head of the famous monastery of St. Thomas. The prelate wanted to know whether Father Franz had any special students to recommend for admission to the Augustinian order of monks. Some of the most talented students of philosophy, mathematics, music, and science had become members of the order and lived at the monastery, which was located at Altbrünn near the city of Brünn, Austria, now shown on modern maps as Brno, Czechoslovakia.

"You are the only one of my students I would recommend for the high honor of joining the monastery of St. Thomas," said Father Franz.

"Do you mean that I could become a priest?" Johann asked in surprise. "My mother would like that, but I have always thought of becoming a teacher or a scientist."

Father Franz told Johann that after he had become ordained as a priest, he could teach or follow whatever talents he had for science. "In the meantime," he added, "you will get a fine education at the monastery without worrying about food or clothing or housing. All the necessities will be provided."

"How wonderful!" Johann said. "Do you think they will accept me?"

Father Franz sent a letter to Prelate Napp strongly recommending Johann. On October 9, 1843, Johann was accepted as a novice, or trial member, of the Augustinian order. According to custom, he took a new name, Brother Gregor Johann Mendel. Today his middle name, Johann, is seldom used, and he is usually referred to as Gregor Mendel.

Life at
the Monastery

The monastery of St. Thomas was built in 1359, almost
five hundred years before Mendel began his training.
Many Augustinian monks who had lived there were noted
for work in science and education. Some taught at famous
universities, such as Oxford, Paris, Vienna, Prague, and
Heidelberg. The monastery prided itself on its fine library
containing about twenty thousand books. And Gregor
Mendel spent many hours studying there.

Mendel made friends with several brilliant monks—
Father Paul Křížkovský, a fine musician, only two years

older than he; Father Franz Bratranek, who was a serious
student of literature, botany, and geology; and Father
Franz Klacel, a devoted astronomer. They gave Mendel
stimulating companionship and helped him get accustomed
to life at the monastery.

In a short time Mendel felt at ease at St. Thomas. He
particularly enjoyed strolling through the beautiful gar-
dens of the monastery with Father Bratranek, discussing
plants. Bratranek pointed out many rare plants which had
been raised by Father Thaler who had been responsible for
the fine botanical garden before his death.

"Father Thaler was a great botanist," said Bratranek. "He

made many interesting experiments with plants in this garden."

Gregor said shyly, "I also like to experiment with plants."

"Perhaps you will carry on with your own experiments in our botanical garden."

Gregor's eyes lighted up. "I could not wish for anything more exciting."

For four years Gregor Mendel devoted himself to preparing for the priesthood. In addition to religion and philosophy he was required to study several languages, among them Czech, Hebrew, Greek, Arabic, Chaldaic, and Syriac. He completed his studies in June, 1848, with a rating of "superexcellent." And at the age of twenty-five he was assigned as a priest in a local parish.

It did not take long for Father Gregor Mendel to find out that he was not suited to the life of a parish priest. He could not bear to hear the sad troubles of people without suffering intensely himself. He reacted to others' feelings so deeply that he actually became ill. Instead of forcing Mendel to continue in parish work, Prelate Napp decided to give him a teaching assignment.

This was a great day for Gregor Mendel. At last his dream had come true. He would be a teacher.

His first job was temporary at the high school in the city of Znaim, forty miles northwest of Vienna. He proved to be a very good teacher, popular with his pupils and the

22

other teachers. But in order to continue teaching permanently, he would have to pass government examinations and receive a certificate.

Unfortunately Mendel did not have enough formal training in the sciences to pass the examinations, and to his great disappointment he failed. One of the examiners, however, was impressed with Mendel. He wrote a letter to Prelate Napp strongly recommending that Mendel be sent to the University of Vienna to study.

Mendel spent from 1851 to 1853 at the University of Vienna at the expense of the monastery. He studied physics, mathematics, botany, zoology, and philosophy. Upon completion of his studies, he returned to the monastery. He became a teacher at the new Modern School at Brünn but he still did not have a teaching certificate. So he took the examinations again. What a blow it was to fail a second time! Nevertheless he continued to teach physics and natural history at the Modern School for more than fifteen years, always on a temporary basis. Whenever he had free time, he spent it in the garden of the monastery experimenting with plants.

Mendel's pupils loved him because he made learning interesting and fun. He took his students on excursions to the woods, where they could observe and dig up rare plants for study. At these times Mendel did not wear his usual monk's habit, but instead wore a frock coat, high

hat, and high boots with his trousers tucked into them, so he could wade through marshes and creeks.

Often he would take his pupils to the botanical garden at the monastery to show them his experiments with flowers. Using the plants as examples, he explained the process involved in seed-bearing and how the seeds when planted would eventually produce offspring.

Mendel probably taught them some of the following facts about plants.

In most flowers both the female and male reproductive organs are within the same blossom. The taller stick at the center of the flower is the female organ called the *pistil*. The bulging part at the bottom of the pistil is the *ovary* which contains the female cells. The thin threadlike stems surrounding the pistil are the male organs, or *stamens*. In order for seeds which will be capable of producing offspring to form, the egg cells in the ovary must be fertilized by male cells called *sperm*. The sperm cells are produced by the stamens and are contained in the powdery yellow grains called *pollen*. Egg cells which are not fertilized by sperm are unable to produce a new generation.

Sex cells are different from the millions of other tiny

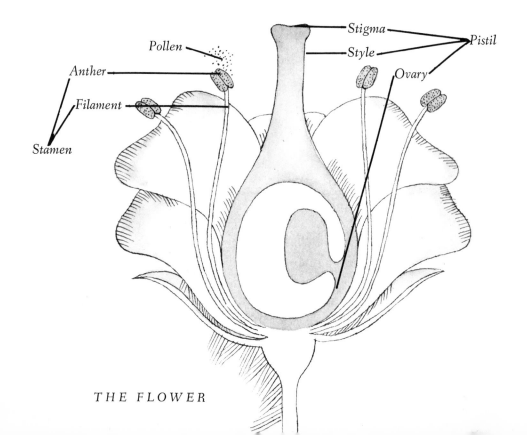

THE FLOWER

cells of which all living things are composed. They are not formed at birth as are the other cells, such as bone, muscle, or skin cells. The sex cells form when young plants are ready to reproduce. Male and female sex cells have the special purpose of combining to produce young.

Mendel did not actually have any scientific knowledge of how sex cells combine with each other. He formed his opinions from observing the results of his experiments with plants. Amazingly his simple conclusions have been proved correct by modern scientists.

In order to understand how the sex cells in a plant combine, let's examine one of the stamens in the diagram. The thin stem of the stamen is called a *filament,* and the little ball at the top of it is called an *anther.* The anther is covered with yellow pollen. Each tiny grain of pollen contains sperm. Now you may ask how does the sperm reach the female cells or eggs in the ovary? Notice the little ball at the top of the pistil. It is called the *stigma.* The slim stem going from the stigma to the ovary is the *style.* The stigma is covered with a sticky substance. Usually the wind or an insect carries pollen from the anther to the stigma. Soon a pollen grain begins to grow a tube down the style into the ovary. The sperm travels down this protective tube and combines with the egg cell. Thus the egg becomes fertilized. It will develop into a seed, which will grow into a plant.

Mendel also showed his students some flowers he was *cross-fertilizing* in order to combine the characteristics of two different varieties of the same plant. Instead of allowing the pollen to fertilize its own flower, Mendel performed a delicate operation. He cut away the stamens of one flower. Then with a little brush he removed pollen from a stamen of another variety of flower in the same family. He brushed the pollen onto the stigma of the first flower, then covered the flower with a little cloth bag so that no unwanted pollen could settle on it. He kept careful records so that he would know exactly which two flowers he had cross-fertilized. Then he watched to see what kind of plant would appear. Would the color of the flower be the same as its mother's or its father's? Would the plant be tall like its father or short like its mother? Would it have long narrow leaves like its father or short wide leaves like its mother?

Mendel's students were fascinated with his experiments and returned often to watch the results. But their teacher never mentioned the serious experiments he had been carrying on for several years with ordinary garden peas. His ideas about them were just beginning to take shape. It would take several more years to learn all the facts he wanted to know, and how the results of his work with peas might be related to other living things.

28

Mendel's
Experiments with Peas

Why do children often resemble their parents? Why should one child inherit eyes like his mother's while another child in the same family inherits a nose like his father's? Why do some children look more like their grandparents, uncles, or aunts than they do like their mothers or fathers? How do children inherit talents and other traits? These were just a few of the questions which puzzled Gregor Mendel. Other scientists had wondered about the same things and had done some experiments with plants and animals. But it seemed that none of them had carried their experiments far enough to provide the answers to these basic questions about how traits are passed from parents to offspring. Today this branch of science is called *genetics*. The word is derived from the Greek *gene,* meaning descent.

Mendel felt sure that there must be a reason for the method by which heredity operates in living things. What were the secrets of nature which no one had as yet uncovered? He thought about his experiments in cross-fertilizing flowers. Suppose he took one kind of plant and cross-fertilized it with a plant of the same species, but which had opposing traits—for instance, tall plants with short plants? What would happen if he then planted the seeds of these cross-fertilized plants for several generations, one after the other? Might he find the answers he was seeking about heredity? He decided to try this even if it took thousands of experiments and many years. A true scientist, Mendel had plenty of patience.

But which plant should he choose for his experiments? After some thought, he decided to use the common garden pea. (The peas we eat are the seeds of the pea plant.) The seeds are cheap and plentiful and come in many varieties. Some peas are round, others are wrinkled; some are green, and some are yellowish; there are also variations in the color of the seed leaves as well as other different characteristics.

Mendel's Experiments with Peas

Mendel decided upon the seven most popular kinds of peas, and he chose an opposite kind for each. Then he could cross-fertilize each kind of plant with the plant that had the opposing trait. This is how he chose the peas with opposing traits, which he called *unit characters:*

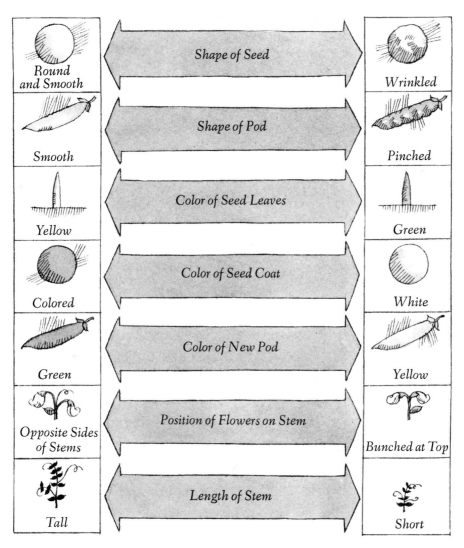

Round and Smooth	Shape of Seed	Wrinkled
Smooth	Shape of Pod	Pinched
Yellow	Color of Seed Leaves	Green
Colored	Color of Seed Coat	White
Green	Color of New Pod	Yellow
Opposite Sides of Stems	Position of Flowers on Stem	Bunched at Top
Tall	Length of Stem	Short

Mendel bought the pea seeds from nearby farmers and seedmen. He asked each grower if the seeds were pure-bred. A purebred seed comes from a plant that has never been cross-fertilized. All the offspring from purebred seeds will have traits like the parent plant. If, for example, the purebred seeds come from a tall parent plant then all the offspring should be tall.

Mendel had to have purebred seeds to begin his experiments in order to be able to recognize what happened when he cross-fertilized them. The seedmen always told him that their seeds were indeed purebred. But Mendel, as a scientist, could not just take their word for it. He had to find out for himself. He planted these seeds and checked the resulting plants to see if they had produced the same characteristics as their parent plants.

In order to make it easy to compare the plants when they were grown, Mendel planted each variety of seed next to the one with the opposite trait. For instance, he planted seeds of tall pea plants next to seeds of short pea plants, round seeds next to wrinkled ones, etc.

It took about eighty days for the pea plants to bear seeds. He studied each plant carefully. Did the seeds of the short plants produce short plants? Did the seeds of the tall plants produce tall plants? He found that usually the plant was what he expected from the seed he had planted. In other words, the seeds were purebred. They had not been cross-fertilized with other kinds of peas. He gathered the purebred seeds and put each kind into a separate jar. He carefully labeled each jar to show what kind of seeds it contained.

Now Mendel wanted to find out whether the seeds would breed true again if he planted them a second time. So the next year he planted the seeds which had been produced by the purebred plants. And sure enough, they did breed true again—tall plants from tall plants, short plants from short plants, etc. Now he was almost sure that if he cross-fertilized these plants, each with its opposite, he would find some of the answers he was seeking about heredity.

In pea plants the pistil (the female organ) and the stamens (the male organs) are contained inside the same closed bud. The tiny anthers at the top of the stamens burst while still inside the bud, covering the pistil with pollen. Thus the seeds become fertilized before the flower opens. This would not do for Mendel's plan. In order to cross-fertilize the plants with their opposites, Mendel had to catch the bud *before the anthers burst*, open the petals of each bud ever so carefully, and snip off the male stamens. Then with a small brush he gathered pollen from the plant with the opposite trait and brushed it onto the pistil of the opened bud.

Mendel had hundreds of plants now. What a slow,

painstaking task it must have been to cross-fertilize each plant with its opposite. But Mendel did not stop there; he also reversed the process. For instance, when he was crossing tall plants with short plants, he brushed pollen from a short plant onto a tall plant; then he did the opposite, brushing pollen from a tall plant onto a short one. He wanted to know whether the way the plants were

crossed would make any difference in the kind of seeds
they produced.

After he cross-fertilized the plants, he put a cloth bag
over each flower. He had to be careful that no other
pollen reached the pistil; otherwise his experiment would
be spoiled.

When the cross-fertilized plants bore seeds, Mendel

gathered them and put them into separate jars with a label on each. These seeds were no longer purebred, but *hybrids*, as they are called today. He had more than a thousand hybrid seeds, each containing two opposing traits, one from each parent. He could hardly wait for the next season to arrive, so he could plant them and see what kinds of plants would appear!

Would the plants grown from the tall-short cross be tall or short? Or would they be middle-sized? And what about the others of the seven kinds of cross-fertilized plants? What would they produce?

Mendel had read papers by other scientists who had experimented with peas. Their results made him suspect that a certain pattern of growth would emerge. Therefore he was not altogether surprised when he found that *all* the plants in the tall-short cross grew *tall*, regardless of whether he had crossed the tall with the short or the short with the tall. Some of these plants were even taller than the tallest of the parent plants. But what had happened to the trait that produced short plants? Had it disappeared forever? He did not think so. He suspected it was just hidden.

In all the seven kinds of crosses he had made, Mendel found that in the first generation of offspring one trait was much stronger than the other. And this stronger trait completely hid its weaker opposite.

Mendel called the stronger trait the *dominant* factor.

Mendel's Experiments with Peas

The trait which seemed to disappear, or at least be held back, he called the *recessive* factor.

He found the following traits were stronger or dominant over the weaker or recessive traits:

DOMINANT		RECESSIVE
Round seeds		Wrinkled seeds
Smooth pods		Pinched pods
Yellow seed leaves		Green seed leaves
Colored seed coats		White seed coats
Green pods		Yellow pods
Flowers alternating on stem		Flowers bunched at top
Tall stems		Short stems

In each group in this first generation of offspring, the dominant trait completely hid the recessive trait. There were only round seeds—no wrinkled ones; only smooth pods—no pinched pods, etc.

Mendel was on his way to finding out some of nature's secrets. What would happen in the next generation? Would the hidden recessive traits reappear? He suspected that they would if the plants were allowed to become *self-fertilized*. Therefore he did not open the buds but allowed them to remain in their natural closed state so that the anthers would burst inside the bud and cover the pistil with pollen, thus allowing each plant to fertilize itself. When the next generation of plants arrived, Mendel found he had been right. In the tall-short group a large number of the plants were tall dominants, but there were also a number of short plants. The recessive trait of shortness had reappeared. And recessive traits were evident in each of the seven groups.

Now Mendel had a clue to a rule in the heredity of pea plants: *After plants have been cross-fertilized with their opposites, they bear hybrid seeds. When these hybrid seeds are planted, they bear plants which show only the stronger or dominant trait. But when these plants grown from hybrid seeds are allowed to become self-fertilized, their offspring include a large number of plants showing the dominant trait but also a lesser*

Mendel's Experiments with Peas

number showing the recessive trait. In other words, in the first generation after cross-fertilization, the weaker or recessive trait is hidden. But in the next generation it reappears.

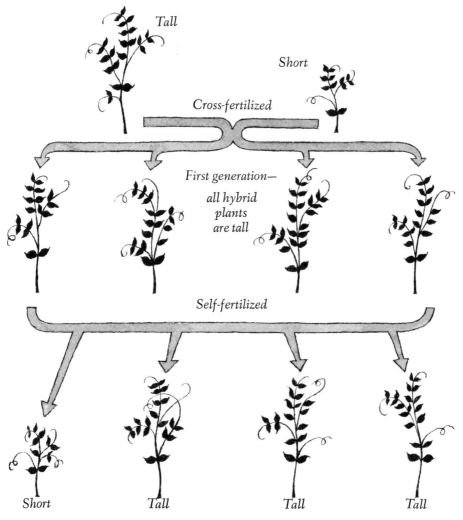

Second generation—one short to three tall plants

This answer was not enough for Mendel's mathematical mind. He had to know what *proportion* of the plants were tall and what proportion were short. And how did the proportion of round seeds compare with the proportion of wrinkled ones?

At this point there were hundreds of plants and thousands of seeds. In order to find out what he wanted to know—the proportion of dominant traits over the proportion of recessive traits—Mendel had to count the number of tall plants and the number of short plants, the number of round seeds and wrinkled seeds, the number of smooth pods and pinched pods, etc. In each of the seven groups he found that the same proportion existed—*three out of four showed the dominant trait. One out of four showed the recessive trait.* Now Mendel was sure there was a definite pattern of inheritance which could be shown mathematically.

But the scientist was still not completely satisfied. Suppose he planted the seeds again and again. What would happen in each future generation? He continued his experiments, and in a few more years he found more facts to support his theory about heredity.

In Mendel's time scientists believed the two different bloods of the parents blended in one stream and the two could never be separated. Why then, Mendel asked himself, when I cross a tall plant with a short one do I get either tall or short plants, never a blend or middle-sized ones? If traits did blend, as scientists thought, Mendel reasoned· there should be plants or seeds showing a mixture of traits inherited from both parents, giving a result that is in between the two parents. It therefore could not be true that the bloods blend. He decided that each trait must always remain in its original form and must be passed on without change. For example, if you had a bag of large lima beans and a bag of small navy beans, you could put them into the same bag and shake them up. But no matter how mixed they became, the large beans would remain large and the small ones small. None would ever become middle-sized. We know today that blood has nothing to do with passing on hereditary traits.

To support his idea further, Mendel made a number of more complicated experiments with peas. Instead of studying a single pair of opposite traits, he studied a combination of two or more in each plant at the same time. He found that regardless of how many opposing traits he crossed, the results in the first generation of offspring were always the same. Only the dominant traits appeared. The recessive traits remained hidden. For instance, when a plant with yellow-round seeds (both dominant traits) was crossed with a plant with green-wrinkled seeds (both recessive traits), all the plants bore only the dominant yellow-round seeds. But when he planted these

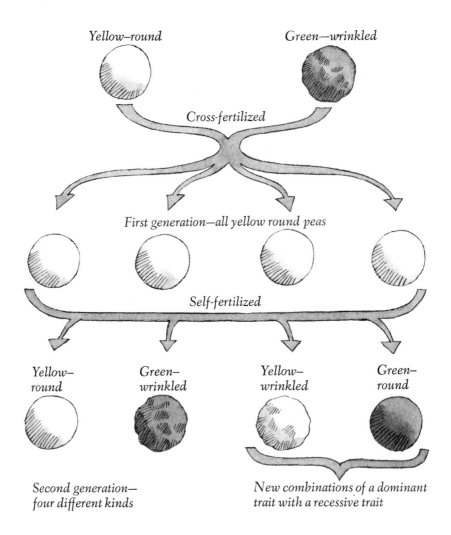

Yellow–round *Green—wrinkled*

Cross-fertilized

First generation—all yellow round peas

Self-fertilized

Yellow–round *Green—wrinkled* *Yellow–wrinkled* *Green–round*

Second generation— four different kinds *New combinations of a dominant trait with a recessive trait*

dominant yellow-round seeds and allowed the plants to become self-fertilized, they bore four different kinds of seeds. The recessive traits had not only reappeared but had combined in a different way to produce two new forms.

How did the two new forms of peas come into existence? This question puzzled Mendel for a long time. At last the answer came to him. *The traits must become separated in some way and then rejoin each other in new combinations.* The more traits, the more possible combinations there could be. He worked out the many possibilities with mathematical formulas. No one had ever before used mathematics to deal with heredity.

During the next eight years Mendel experimented with ten thousand plants. It was becoming more and more clear to him that a child might inherit some traits from his father, some from his mother, and still others from a grandfather or grandmother. In human beings there may be as many as a thousand different traits, and the possible combinations can run into the millions. A recessive trait may lie hidden for many generations before it reappears.

At last Mendel was ready to present his ideas to his fellow scientists.

Mendel
Reads His Report

On February 8, 1865, Mendel read the first half of a long, detailed report on his experiments with peas before the Natural History Society of Brünn. And a month later he read the latter half of the report. The points of the two reports may be summed up briefly as follows:

1.   Unit characteristics or traits in pea plants appear in opposing forms such as tall or short, round or wrinkled seeds, smooth pod or pinched pod, etc.

2.   Each trait in a living thing is decided by a pair

of inherited factors—one from each parent. (Today these factors are called *genes*.)

3. In a plant grown from hybrid seeds, some traits are much stronger than others. The stronger traits are called *dominant*. The weaker traits are called *recessive*. The dominant traits can completely hide the recessive traits but not change them. The recessive traits may reappear in a later generation. (Today this is known as Mendel's Law of Dominance and Recessiveness.)

4. When a growing plant is ready for mating, it forms both male and female sex cells for the express purpose of producing offspring. At this time the two inherited factors for each trait separate from each other. Only one factor for each trait remains in each sex cell, male or female. (Today the term *segregation* is used to describe this process.)

5. After segregation has taken place, one male cell unites with one female cell, and the egg becomes fertilized. Due to segregation each sex cell carries only one factor for each trait. When they join each other, the seed again contains two factors for each trait, one from each parent. But the traits do not necessarily pair off in the same combination that existed in the parents. They may combine in many ways, resulting in a variety of offspring. (Today the term *recombination* is used to describe this process.)

6. When more than one pair of inherited traits is involved, each trait behaves as a unit and is inherited independently of other traits. For example, seed color is not influenced by the seed being round or wrinkled, and inheritance of height is independent of inheritance of seed color. (Today this is known as Mendel's Law of Independent Assortment.)

Most of the scientists who had come to hear Mendel's report were friends who had helped him organize the Natural History Society. There were about forty men present at each meeting. They all listened politely and applauded at the end. But Mendel could feel a decided lack of enthusiasm. Although time was allowed for discussion, no one cared enough to even ask a question.

47

Just a few years earlier, in 1859, the famous book, *The Origin of Species*, by Charles Darwin, had been published. In this book the great naturalist had pointed out that all living things pass on traits, or as he called them "variations," to their offspring. It was Darwin's idea that variations are passed on without interruption from one generation to the next. He admitted, however, that he did not know how changes in species were brought about. (Unfortunately Darwin was not familiar with Mendel's scientific experiments.)

Charles Darwin

Most of the world's scientists were impressed with Darwin's ideas, yet no one among those assembled at the Brünn society realized that Mendel was supplying the missing link to Darwin's theory. In the explanation of dominant and recessive traits, Mendel was pointing out that evolution is not a smooth, continuous operation, but one which is interrupted by recessive factors which reappear in later generations. And in his explanation of segregation and recombination he was supplying the answer to how heredity operates. No one had any idea that Mendel was making one of the greatest contributions to natural science.

In spite of the fact that the report had created no great excitement, the editor of the journal, *Proceedings of the Brünn Society,* offered to publish Mendel's findings. The journal was exchanged with more than a hundred other scientific societies around the world.

Mendel was delighted and full of new hope! Now scientists in other countries would read his report. Surely some of them would be interested in his work. His report was published under the title "Experiments in Plant Hybridization."

After publication of his report, Mendel watched his mail hopefully for a long, long time. But no one anywhere recognized his work sufficiently to even write him a letter about it.

Disappointed as he was, Mendel continued his research. Now he resumed some earlier experiments with hawkweed, a form of dandelion. For some reason which Mendel was unable to figure out, the hawkweed did not breed true, and did not lend itself to a mathematical formula as the peas had. He studied the published papers of other scientists about hawkweed hybrids. The most outstanding ones were those of a renowned professor at the University of Munich, Karl von Nägeli.

Mendel had an idea. Why not write a letter to the famous professor asking his advice on his hawkweed experiments and at the same time call the great scientist's attention to his own published paper on peas? If the professor were impressed, he might bring Mendel's theories to the attention of his students and even other scientists.

In the fall of 1866, Mendel wrote Professor von Nägeli and enclosed a copy of his paper, "Experiments in Plant Hybridization." At least two months passed before Mendel received a reply. Alas, the professor showed no sign of interest in Mendel's pea experiments. He only encouraged Mendel to continue his work using hawkweeds. Mendel did this and carried on a correspondence with Nägeli for several years. Unfortunately the hawkweeds did not breed according to expectations, and the experiments were doomed to failure. Some present-day scientists have read the correspondence between Mendel and Nägeli and can find no logical reason why Nägeli failed to be interested in Mendel's pea experiments.

Three years went by, and at times it seemed to Mendel that his eight years of hard, serious work with pea plants had been completely wasted. He must have had many doubts. Was his report a failure because he had confined himself to the humble pea plant instead of using some rare flower? Since most scientists at that time were not interested in mathematics, might they have been bored with his mathematical approach to heredity? Or was it merely that his friends did not take him seriously as a scientist? Whatever the reasons might be, Mendel could not help feeling that some day his work would be recognized. He kept insisting to his friends, "My time will come . . . my time will come."

Mendel's
Surprise Honor

In 1886, just three years after Mendel's report to the Natural History Society, Prelate Cyrill Napp, the head of St. Thomas monastery, died, after serving the monastery for forty-four years. His death was a great loss to the whole community as well as to the monks of St. Thomas. It was necessary for the monks to hold an election to choose a successor from among their own group. But who could take Prelate Napp's place?

"We must choose someone who can make wise business decisions," said Father Křížkovský. "He will have to be able to handle the affairs of the large estates and the dairy farms owned by the monastery."

"He should be a young man who can serve for a long time," said Father Bratranek, "since a large tax must be paid to the state each time a new prelate is elected."

"He must be able to get along with many kinds of people," said Father Klacel.

"I hope he will be someone who is open-minded and has a strong feeling for education, the arts, and sciences," said Gregor Mendel. "He will have to serve on many committees."

On March 30, 1868, the election took place. And when the votes were counted, Father Gregor Mendel was stunned to find that he had been chosen Abbot and Prelate of St. Thomas monastery. It never occurred to him that he could be worthy of such a great honor. If only his mother and father could have seen him installed in his new office. What a proud moment this would have been! But both his parents had died—his father in 1857 and his mother in 1861. However, his two sisters and their families were thrilled with Mendel's good fortune. Theresia, the sister who had helped him by giving up her dowry, was overjoyed, but no more than he was. Now he could afford to pay for educating her three sons. To repay Theresia was one of the greatest pleasures of his life.

At first after taking his new post at the age of forty-six, Mendel tried to continue with some of his experiments. But he soon found that the duties of running the business affairs of the monastery, in addition to his many civic duties, took all his time and energy.

He had a comfortable suite in the monastery and often on Sunday afternoons entertained many important friends —among them scientists, judges, and state officers. Often Theresia's sons came to visit him, and these were the happiest times of all.

Perhaps because he had been so hungry in his youth, Prelate Mendel became a heavy eater and gained more and more weight. Soon he was troubled by heart and kidney disease. Finally in the summer of 1883, after fifteen years of service as Prelate, he had to spend many months in bed. He turned over the business affairs of the monastery to Father Ambros Poje.

On Sunday, January 6, 1884, Gregor Mendel died at the age of sixty-two. Many people of all faiths attended the funeral. Everyone felt the loss of the kind, charitable Prelate. But only a few of his close friends knew of his experiments in heredity. Eighteen years had passed since his paper, "Experiments in Plant Hybridization," had been published. Although he had predicted "my time will come," he died not knowing that it actually would.

Mendel
Is Discovered

Gregor Mendel's great contributions to the study of heredity went unrecognized until sixteen years after his death. Thirty-four years had passed since the publication of his paper in the "Proceedings." Then the world was suddenly awakened to his remarkable work.

In 1900 three botanists in different parts of Europe called the world's attention to the great scientist who had been so many years ahead of his time.

In March the Dutch botanist, Hugo de Vries, published two papers about experiments with hybrid primroses. He mentioned that after completing his experiments, he wanted to find out what other scientists had done along the same lines. In his research he came across a paper written thirty-four years earlier by an Augustinian monk named Gregor Mendel. He was surprised to find that although Mendel's experiments had been carried on with garden peas, the monk's conclusions were strikingly similar to his own.

In April, a German botanist, Carl Correns, who had been experimenting with pea hybrids, published a paper entitled, "Gregor Mendel's rules concerning the Behavior of Racial Hybrids." He praised Mendel's work highly and stated that the monk's experiments and results closely resembled his own as well as those of De Vries.

Then in June, Erich Tschermak, an Austrian botanist, published a paper on pea hybrids and also paid tribute to Gregor Mendel.

This enthusiastic praise of Mendel from three different sources within a few months created excitement among scientists all around the world. The study of heredity was greatly increased by those who wished to prove or disprove Mendel's findings. Thus the new science of *genetics* was born.

Mendel's five principles of heredity are often referred to as the *Mendelian laws*. Although new high-powered microscopes and advanced research methods have revealed

Walther Flemming

exceptions to Mendel's rules, these laws are still the foundation of modern genetics.

One of the most important modifications of Mendel's laws was the discovery that traits are not passed on to offspring one by one, as Mendel believed. In 1879 a German scientist, Walther Flemming, observed with a new high-powered microscope that cells divide and duplicate themselves. He also observed thin threadlike rods in the nucleus of each cell. He called these *chromosomes*, meaning "colored bodies" because when he stained the tissue, these rods in the nucleus became visible.

It was not until 1902 that another giant step was taken in the science of genetics. William S. Sutton, an American biologist, suggested that each chromosome carried a set of many genes. Later scientists found that the chromosomes in cells are arranged in pairs. One member of each pair is inherited from the male parent and the other member from the female parent. Each chromosome contains a group of genes. The number of pairs of chromosomes in each cell varies in different living things. A pea plant has seven pairs in each cell; a fruit fly has four pairs; and a human being has twenty-three pairs.

In a pea plant, for example, the seven pairs in each cell separate during the formation of reproductive cells, leaving each egg cell or each sperm cell with seven single chromosomes. When a male cell unites with a female cell at the time of fertilization, each brings its seven chromosomes which combine into seven pairs again, each of the fourteen chromosomes having its individual set of genes. (The chromosomes do not necessarily combine into the same pairs that existed in the parent plant.)

In view of these observations Mendel's theory of *segregation and recombination* has been wholly accepted in modern genetics, the only difference being that instead of each pair of *genes* separating and re-uniting in new combinations, each pair of *chromosomes* does so, carrying its own set of a variety of genes.

60

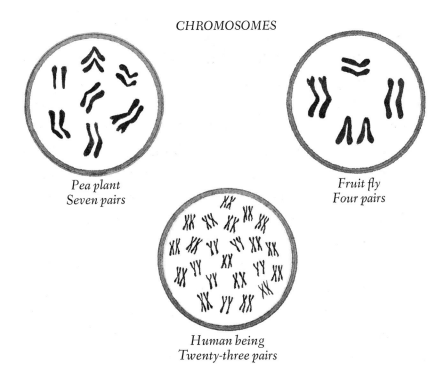

Pea plant
Seven pairs

Fruit fly
Four pairs

Human being
Twenty-three pairs

One of the great discoveries in modern genetics was the fact that a gene occasionally becomes changed and does not produce the trait normally expected. Such changes in genes may come about when reproductive cells are overexposed to radiation or to certain chemicals. These changes, known as *mutations*, produce defective genes which cause abnormalities or diseases when inherited by the offspring. Such a hereditary change may not appear in the immediate offspring, since it may be a recessive trait hidden by a dominant gene, but it usually appears in a later generation.

Most mutations are harmful, causing the offspring receiving the "genetic mistake" to be less able to survive in his environment or to be deformed in some way. Some examples of conditions caused by defective genes resulting from mutations are wingless flies, human beings with six fingers on one or both hands, a disease known as *hemophilia* in which a person's blood does not clot normally, and *albinism* (a lack of color pigmentation in the skin, eyes, and hair.)

Knowing about harmful mutations has greatly benefited mankind. Using Mendel's laws, scientists can predict mathematically how many offspring are likely to inherit a defect from parents. By proper selection of breeding stock, farmers can often prevent the possibility of parents passing on an undesirable trait. Thus farmers are able to breed better poultry, cattle, and other animals.

Genetics has also aided in breeding disease-resistant varieties of livestock. It has been of great value as well in improving the quality of vegetables, cereals, and other plants.

Heredity
in Human Beings

One of the most famous research projects in genetics was initiated in 1910 by Dr. Thomas Hunt Morgan, a zoologist at Columbia University in New York City.

Dr. Morgan wished to study how Mendel's laws apply to heredity in human beings. Since the action of chromosomes and genes is basically the same in almost all living things, Dr. Morgan decided to use the tiny fruit fly for his experiments. This little fly, which can be seen buzzing around a bunch of bananas, can produce as many as two hundred offspring in two weeks, or about twenty-five generations in each year, as opposed to human beings, who produce only one generation in approximately twenty years. Another point in favor of using the fruit fly for the experiments was the fact that it has only four pairs of chromosomes per cell; human beings have twenty-three pairs per cell. Thus it was easier to study the fruit fly under the microscope.

Dr. Morgan and his associates carried out the fruit-fly research for more than two decades with remarkable results. Dr. Morgan's work was recognized in 1933, when he was awarded the Nobel prize in medicine. His research established that Mendel's mathematical pattern of heredity and his theory of dominant and recessive factors do indeed apply to human beings. And even more important the Morgan team discovered that certain chromosomes are responsible for determining whether offspring will be male or female. They named these the "X" and "Y" chromosomes.

You will remember that pairs of chromosomes separate from each other at the time of formation of reproductive cells. Originally, a female cell has two X chromosomes, or XX. A male cell, on the other hand, has two unlike chromosomes, one X and one Y, thus XY. By studying mature egg cells, the researchers found that after the separation process has taken place, each female cell is left with only one X chromosome instead of two, while each male or

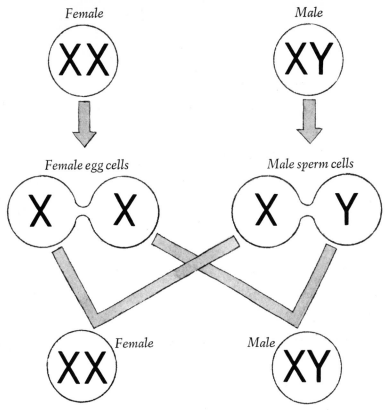

Female

Male

XX

XY

Female egg cells

Male sperm cells

X   X

X   Y

Female

Male

XX

XY

Female "X" combined with male "X" results in "XX" producing female offspring

Female "X" combined with male "Y" results in "XY" producing male offspring

sperm cell contains only X alone or Y alone. (The original XY cell produces 50 percent X chromosomes and 50 percent Y.)

You will recall also that after the chromosomes have separated, a recombination takes place. Thus either a male X or Y chromosome may combine with the female X. Many experiments showed that if the egg was fertilized by a male X chromosome, it then again contained two X's, one from each parent, or XX. The offspring with the XX

65

combination always turned out to be female. But if a Y chromosome fertilized the egg, making an XY combination, a male was born. (There are more complicated combinations of X and Y chromosomes in various living things, but generally the condition described prevails.)

Morgan and his colleagues also observed that certain defective genes are passed from the male parent to his female offspring, usually remaining recessive in the female. She in turn, however, passes on the defective genes to her son. The characteristics that these genes produce in the offspring are called *sex-linked traits*. One example of a sex-linked trait is color blindness, which prevents a person from distinguishing red from green. You will recall that the pair of chromosomes determining a female is XX and the pair producing a male is XY. The gene for color blindness is recessive, and like some other defective genes, is carried only on the X chromosome, which is larger than the Y. For a female (XX) to be color-blind, she would have to inherit *two* recessive genes for the trait. If she received even one dominant gene for normal color vision, it would cancel the recessive gene and she would not be color-blind. But a male (XY) has no gene for color vision on his Y chromosome, and would therefore be color-blind if he inherited only one recessive gene for color blindness on his X chromosome. This condition is therefore more common among men than women.

A serious disease caused by defective genes is *hemophilia,* which is also transmitted by the female to her male off-spring. The blood of a male with hemophilia does not clot properly so that he might bleed to death from even a minor cut or bruise.

A remarkable new advance now enables doctors to determine the sex of a baby six months before it is born. In the case where a family may be subject to hemophilia or other serious defects, this early detection can be a great boon in planning immediate treatment at birth, or in some instances even before birth.

Genetics
Today

One of the greatest steps forward in the science of genetics was the discovery of an acid found in the nucleus of each cell (aptly called *nucleic* acid). Usually this chemical is referred to by the initials DNA, which stand for deoxyribonucleic acid.

The existence of DNA was first noted in 1868 (during Mendel's lifetime) by a Swiss scientist named Friederich Miescher. Mendel had no knowledge of Miescher's work, and though some modern geneticists were acquainted with it, they attached very little significance to DNA as related to heredity.

Genetics Today

A revolution in biology took place in 1946, when a research project begun at Rockefeller Institute in New York brought forth evidence that genes are made of DNA. Up to that time, the question "What are genes made of?" had puzzled scientists but had gone unanswered.

DNA, like all chemical substances, is composed of molecules. A wonderful aid in the study of DNA was a construction of a diagram of its molecules and an explanation of how they function. In 1962 the Nobel prize for this accomplishment was shared by an Englishman, Francis Compton Crick, and his American associate, James Dewey Watson, who worked together at Cambridge University in England.

The DNA molecule, as described by Crick and Watson, is shaped like a ladder which has been twisted like a spring or corkscrew. The steps of the ladder are composed of four different chemicals, two of which join to make each rung. The order in which these four chemicals occur determines the particular code of genetic information. You can see that even with only four code letters, it is possible to have thousands of different arrangements. As different sequences result in different genetic traits, we begin to understand why the living things around us show such varying characteristics.

The amount of DNA in a fertilized human egg is so small that it weighs only about two ten-trillionths of an ounce. Nevertheless it determines the thousands of traits a child can inherit.

In addition to determining hereditary traits, it was found that DNA directs the building of proteins, which do hundreds of jobs in the construction and functioning of the cells. It is not yet fully understood how DNA contributes to protein building, but generally speaking, DNA manufactures in the nucleus another chemical, called RNA or ribonucleic acid. RNA acts as an assistant to DNA in the complicated process of building proteins.

Both DNA and RNA have been created artificially in the laboratory. The Nobel prize for this work was shared in 1959 by Dr. Arthur Kornberg of Stanford University and Dr. Severo Ochoa of New York University. Since then, great strides have been made in biology and other related sciences as well as genetics.

Scientists have been able to produce new hereditary traits in bacteria and insects. Many geneticists believe that it will not be too long before they will be able to alter the DNA in human eggs and sperm cells, replacing defective genes with normal ones, thus saving future generations from feeble-mindedness, deaf-mutism, and many other deformities or illnesses. However, the power to control heredity could be used for evil as well as for good. Suppose a mad genius decided to create a generation of science-fiction monsters or a race of supermen without moral responsibility. It is important that society insist upon certain controls over genetic experimentation.

In addition to the study of DNA in relation to the body, studies have also been made of its relation to mental activity. Another modern study suggests that criminal behavior may be influenced by abnormal chromosomes. A number of male criminals have been found to have an extra Y chromosome—instead of the normal combination, which is *XY*, these men have *XYY* chromosomes. They are apparently more aggressive and commit crimes without motives more readily. Based on this condition, a plea of "not guilty because of insanity" has been entered in murder cases. This study is still new, and there is a great difference of opinion, however, about how much the *XYY* chromosomes may be held responsible for a man's criminal acts.

An important new development in genetics was reported in 1969 by Nobel prize-winning scientist Har Gobind Khorana, who was associated with the University of Wisconsin at that time. He reported progress in trying to create a *gene*, the basic unit in the blueprint for life, in the laboratory. Khorana and two associates presented a scientific paper to the Federation of American Societies for Experimental Biology revealing that they have been able to create two-thirds of a small gene found in yeast cells. They hope to

71

be able to create an entire gene. Perhaps by the time you read this, their goal will have been reached.

   In spite of the remarkable new developments in genetics in laboratories all over the world, scientists are quick to give great credit to the humble monk, Gregor Mendel, for the basic elements of this fascinating science. In 1910 scientists all over the world contributed funds to the erection of a beautiful statue of Mendel. It stands today in Brünn, a memorial honoring the father of genetics.

Glossary

ANTHER a little ball at the top of the stamen (male sex organ) of a flower.

CHROMOSOME a thin threadlike rod in the nucleus of each cell.

CROSS-FERTILIZE to transfer pollen from one plant to another plant with opposing characteristics.

DNA deoxyribonucleic acid. The substance that genes are made of, found in the nucleus of cells.

DOMINANT TRAITS stronger genetic traits of an organism.

EGG the female cell contained in the ovary of a flower.

GENETICS the science that studies how traits are passed from parents to offspring.

73

HEREDITY   the process in which parents pass traits on to offspring.

HYBRID   a plant which results from selective cross-fertilization.

MUTATION   a chemical change in genes causing abnormalities.

OVARY   in flowers, a sac at the bottom of the pistil containing the female egg cells.

PISTIL   the female sex organ of a flower.

POLLEN   powdery yellow grains containing sperm cells.

RECESSIVE TRAITS   weaker or hidden genetic traits.

RNA   ribonucleic acid. An organic substance produced in the nucleus of cells.

SEGREGATION   the process by which chromosomes separate and recombine in a reproductive cell.

SELF-FERTILIZATION   nature's method by which pollen is carried from the male anthers of a flower to its female pistil, allowing the flower to fertilize itself.

SPERM   the male sexual cell.

STAMENS   several thin threadlike stems which constitute the male sex organs of a flower.

STIGMA   a little ball at the top of the pistil (female sex organ) of a flower.

STYLE   the slim stem going from the stigma to the ovary of the pistil (female sex organ) of a flower.

UNIT CHARACTERISTICS   natural traits in a plant.

74

Books About
Gregor Mendel and Genetics

FOR YOUNG READERS

GREENE, CARLA *Charles Darwin.* New York: The Dial Press, 1968.

RANDAL, JUDITH *All About Heredity.* New York: Random House, Inc., 1963.

SOOTIN, HARRY *Gregor Mendel, Father of the Science of Genetics.* New York: The Vanguard Press, Inc., 1959.

WEBSTER, GARY *The Man Who Found Out Why,* the Story of Gregor Mendel. New York: Hawthorne Books, 1962.

FOR OLDER READERS

BEADLE, GEORGE W., AND MURIEL BEADLE *The Language of·Life.* Garden City: Doubleday & Co., 1966.

GOLDSTEIN, PHILLIP *Triumphs of Biology.* Garden City: Doubleday & Co., 1965.

GOLDSTEIN, PHILLIP *Genetics Is Easy.* New York: Lantern Press, Inc., revised edition, 1967.

HAFFNER, RUDOLPH E. *Genetics, The Thread of Life.* Columbus: American Education Publications, 1962.

ILTIS, HUGO *Life Of Mendel.* New York: Hafner Publishing Co., Inc., 1966.

MONTAGU, ASHLEY *Human Heredity.* Cleveland: World Publishing Co., 1959.

SCHEINFELD, AMRAM *Your Heredity and Environment.* Philadelphia: J. B. Lippincott Co., 1966.

NOTE: *The study of genetics and accomplishments in the field are growing so rapidly that no book can be completely up to date. The student is advised to watch his daily newspapers and leading magazines for advances in this fascinating science.*

Index

77

Index

Natural History Society of Brünn, 44, 47

Ochoa, Dr. Severo, 73
Origin of Species, The (Darwin), 48

Pea plants: experiments with, 28, 29–43; number of chromosomes per cell, 60
Philosophical Institute, 13
Pistil, 26; in pea plants, 33
Plants: cross-fertilization in, 28, 30–43; reproductive organs of, 26; self-fertilization in, 38–39, 42
Poje, Father Ambrose, 56
Pollen, 26, 27, 28; pea plants, 33
Proceedings of the Brünn Society, 49
Proteins, 71, 72–73
Purebred seeds, 32-33

Recessive factor, 36–43, 45, 49, 64
Recombination, 45, 49, 60
Reproductive organs of plants, 26
RNA (ribonucleic acid), 71–73; messenger, 72-73; ribosomal, 72–73; transfer, 72–73
Rockefeller Institute, 69

St. Thomas monastery, 16–18; life at, 19–22; Mendel as Prelate of, 52–56
Schindler, Leopold, 14
Seeds, 26–27; experiments with peas, 28, 29–43; hybrids, 36, 38, 45, 50; purebred, 32–33
Segregation, 45, 49, 60
Self-fertilization, 38–39, 42
Sex cells, 26–27, 45
Sex-linked traits, 66
Sperm cells, 26, 60, 64–66
Stamens, 26, 27, 28; pea plants, 33
Stigma, 27, 28
Sturm, Alois, 13–14
Style, 27
Sutton, William S., 60

Thaler, Father, 20–22
Traits, 44–46; Darwin on, 48; dominant factor, 36–43, 45, 49, 64; Flemming's discovery, 59; hidden, 36; purebred seeds and, 32–33; question of blending, 40–41; recessive factor in, 36–43, 45, 49, 64; sex-linked, 66; Sutton's discovery, 60; unit characters, 31. *See also* Heredity
Tschermak, Erich, 58

Unit characters, 31

Variations, 48
Von Nägeli, Karl, 50–51

Watson, James Dewey, 69

X chromosomes, 64–66

Y chromosomes, 64–66